💬 **Say the sounds:** puff puff, rustle, clatter, knock knock, la la la

- Whose birthday do you think it is?

- What do you think Kipper is saying?

1

💬 **Say the sounds:** ding dong, shake shake, come in, meow, raaah!

● What sort of music do you think they're listening to? Can you hum the tune?

● What do you think is inside Kipper's present?

3

4

Say the sounds: rip rip, click, hoot, lick, bang

- How many children can you count at the party?

- What other party games can you think of? What noises would you hear during them?

5

💬 **Say the sounds:** slurp, crunch, snap, hee hee, pop

- What sound do you think the jelly makes as Mum scoops it up?

- Why do you think Kipper is laughing?

- Which song is everyone singing? Let's sing along!
- What will Kipper do next?